50

fantastic things to do with
Babies

SALLY AND PHILL FEATHERSTONE

BULK PURCHASE

Gryphon House books are available for special premiums and sales promotions as well as for fund-raising use. Special editions or book excerpts also can be created to specification. For details, contact the Director of Marketing at Gryphon House.

DISCLAIMER

Gryphon House, Inc., and the authors cannot be held responsible for damage, mishap, or injury incurred during the use of or because of activities in this book. Appropriate and reasonable caution and adult supervision of children involved in activities and corresponding to the age and capability of each child involved is recommended at all times. Do not leave children unattended at any time. Observe safety and caution at all times.

50 Fantastic Things to Do With Babies

Gryphon House, Inc.
Lewisville, NC

SALLY AND PHILL FEATHERSTONE

50 FANTASTIC THINGS TO DO WITH BABIES

by Sally and Phill Featherstone

COPYRIGHT

© 2013 Gryphon House, Inc.
Published by Gryphon House, Inc. P.O. Box 10, Lewisville, NC 27023
800.638.0928 (phone); 877.638.7576 (fax).
Visit us on the web at www.gryphonhouse.com

Originally published in 2010 by A&C Black Publishers Limited.

LIBRARY OF CONGRESS

CATALOGING-IN-PUBLICATION INFORMATION:

Featherstone, Sally.
 50 fantastic things to do with babies / by Sally and Phill Featherstone.
     pages cm
 "Originally published in 2010 by A&C Black Publishers Limited"--Publisher's note.
 Includes index.
 ISBN 978-0-87659-463-6
1. Infants--Development. 2. Education, Preschool--Activity programs. 3. Education, Preschool--Parent participation. 4. Play. I. Featherstone, Phill. II. Title. III. Title: Fifty fantastic things to do with babies.
 HQ774.F43 2013
 372.21--dc23
                          2012044469

Contents

Introduction

There's plenty of research to show that babies and children who enjoy a stimulating home environment learn better and more quickly. So what parents and caregivers do to lay the groundwork for learning early on is an investment that pays back throughout the child's life.

This book has been specially written for parents to use with their babies at home. However, it can also be used by caregivers and workers in daycares and child care settings. It contains 50 simple activities that can be done easily with very little equipment, often in your spare time. It's not a course to work through. All the ideas here are suitable for newborns to around 20 months, and in many cases beyond. Some are more suited to younger babies, and some to older. It's obvious which these are. Choose what you and your baby enjoy. When you find an activity you like, do it again and again. Babies love repetition and benefit from it.

Finally, please remember that one of the main aims of this book is fun. There are few things as delightful or rewarding as being alongside young children as they explore, enquire, experiment, and learn. Join them in their enthusiasm for learning, and enjoy being with them!

There are three books in the
50 Fantastic Things series:

50 Fantastic Things to Do with Babies (suitable for use from soon after birth to 20 months)
50 Fantastic Things to Do with Toddlers (suitable for use from 16–36 months)
50 Fantastic Things to Do with Preschoolers (suitable for use from 30–50 months)

The age groupings above are approximate and are only suggestions. Children develop at different speeds. They also grow in spurts, with some periods of rapid development alternating with other times when they don't seem to change as quickly. So don't worry if your baby doesn't seem ready for a particular activity. Try another instead and return to it later. On the other hand, if your baby gets on well and quickly, try some of the ideas in the "Another idea" and "Ready for more?" sections.

A NOTE ON SAFETY

Care must be taken at all times when dealing with babies and young children. Common sense will be your main guide, but here are a few ideas to help you have fun safely.

Babies and young children naturally explore things by bringing them to their mouths. This is fine, but always check that toys and other objects you use are clean.

Although rare, swallowing objects or choking on them is a hazard. Some children are more susceptible than others. If you are concerned about choking, buy a choking tester from a retail baby supply store.

Baby's lungs are delicate. They need clean air. Never smoke near your baby, and don't allow anyone else to do so.

Children are naturally inquisitive, and you will want to encourage this. However, secure and happy children are often unaware of danger. Your baby needs you to watch out for her. Make sure you are always there. You can't watch your baby all the time, but don't leave her alone and unsupervised for more than a few minutes at a time. Even when she is asleep, check on her regularly.

The objects and toys we suggest here have been chosen for their safety. Nevertheless, most things can be dangerous if they go wrong or are not used properly:

- Mobiles and toys tied to baby gyms are great to encourage looking and reaching, but check that they are fastened securely.
- Ribbons and string are fascinating to babies, but they can be a choking hazard. They can also become wrapped around arms, legs, and necks.
- Babies are natural explorers. They need clean floors. Store outdoor shoes away from areas where your baby will be lying and crawling.
- If your baby is just learning to balance, either sitting or standing, make sure he has a soft landing. Put a pillow behind babies who are starting to sit. If your baby is starting to crawl or walk, look out for trip hazards.
- Take care with furniture. Make sure your baby is fastened securely into his high chair. Pad sharp edges of tables and other furniture.

Let's Look
making contact

DID YOU KNOW?
Young babies focus best on faces and objects held between 8–10 inches away.

WHAT YOU NEED:

- No special equipment for this activity.

Ready for more?

Make movements with your lips and mouth. See if your baby copies you. Do the same activity facing a mirror so you can both see both of you.

WHAT TO DO:

1. Sit holding your baby in your lap, facing you. Rest your arms on a cushion if that helps.
2. Make sure your face is near enough for your baby to see you clearly (but not too close).
3. Talk or sing softly to your baby. Watch your baby's face as you do so.
4. As you talk, sometimes open your mouth wide or stick out your tongue. Watch to see if your baby copies your expression.
5. Move your head slowly from side to side, and watch how your baby follows your face with his eyes.
6. Keep talking, singing, and smiling.

Another idea: Put on a hat or a pair of glasses, and try the same activity again.

What is your baby learning?

Contact with you and watching your face is important in learning to talk. As you do this activity more, your baby will probably start to respond by smiling, wriggling, and babbling. Don't worry if this takes time; sometimes he's just not in the mood.

HELPFUL HINTS

It's common for very young babies to have trouble making out objects clearly and focusing on them. Make sure the light is behind your baby and not in his eyes. Change the expressions on your face slowly and hold them for a while. You need to give your baby plenty of time to explore your face with his eyes, and to respond to your expressions.

First Faces
fun with face patterns

WHAT YOU NEED:

- a small paper plate or circle of white cardboard
- a black marker or crayon
- a chopstick, pencil, or wooden spoon for a handle
- some tape or glue

WHAT TO DO:

1. Draw a face on a paper plate or a circle of cardboard. Keep it very simple— eyes and mouth are all that's needed.
2. Glue or tape the face on to a stick.
3. Put your baby in a baby chair or prop her up with a pillow.
4. Hold the face puppet close to the baby's face (8-10" away).
5. Talk to your baby while you move the face slowly from side to side. Only move the face a few centimeters each way. Watch your baby's eyes and slow down or stop if she stops following.
6. If the baby reaches out to touch the face, help by gently guiding her hand.

Ready for more?

Make another face puppet. Glue this one upside down on the stick. Use both puppets and see which face your baby likes best. Glue a plastic toy (a bath duck, plastic car, small doll) on a stick. Play with that in the same way, and see how your baby responds.

Another idea: Draw some more faces with different expressions. Keep them simple.

What is your baby learning?

Playing this game will help your baby recognize faces and movement and will help her focus her eyes. Watch for her to follow your movements and respond to the paper-plate face by making sounds, smiling, or staring.

Hide and Seek
peekaboo, there you are!

WHAT YOU NEED:

- a piece of fabric, thin enough to see through (examples: a net curtain, a piece of voile, a chiffon scarf)

WHAT TO DO:

1. Sit your baby in your lap facing you, or opposite you in a baby chair.
2. Smile and talk to your baby. Tell him about the game.
3. Hold the fabric up between you so your face is hidden. Keep talking or singing.
4. Slowly lower the fabric so you can see each other, saying, "There you are!"
5. Don't go too fast at first—your baby will need time to understand the concept.
6. Now put the fabric right over your head and slowly pull it off, talking all the time.

Another idea: Play the same game again, using thicker fabric, such as a towel.

DID YOU KNOW?

The shape of the human face is the first thing a baby learns to recognize.

Ready for more?

Place the fabric gently over your baby's head and slowly pull it off. Talk all the time. Some babies don't like their faces covered. Stop at once if he becomes agitated. As your baby gets used to the game, use fabrics that are harder to see through.

HELPFUL HINTS

Watch for signs of agitation and stop at once if your baby seems not to be enjoying the activity. Very sheer fabrics can restrict breathing and can be a choking hazard. Do not allow your baby to play with fabric without your close supervision.

What is your baby learning?

Playing this game will help your baby learn to copy and imitate. Look for him to respond by making sounds, smiling, and waving his limbs.

Your baby might need you to take her hands and guide them gently to the objects. Allow your baby plenty of time to lift her head to look and focus.

What is your baby learning?

Playing this game will help your baby learn to copy and imitate. Look for her to respond by making sounds, smiling, and waving her limbs.

Mirror, Mirror
mirrors and shiny objects

WHAT YOU NEED:

- a shallow basket or tray
- a baby's safety mirror
- as many shiny objects as you can find (a metal serving spoon, a pan lid, shiny toys)

Ready for more?

Line a shoebox with shiny paper. Fill it with a selection of different brightly colored objects. Explore the contents with your baby. Stick some black tape to a mirror to make stripes or patterns on the surface.

WHAT TO DO:

1. Clear a space and remove other distractions. Sit your baby in a baby chair or prop her up with a cushion.
2. Place all the shiny objects and the mirror in the basket.
3. Sit opposite your baby and hold the mirror where she can look into it. Tap the mirror to encourage her to reach for it.
4. Sing or chant, "Look (baby's name), who can I see? I can see you!" Tap the reflection and then gently stroke your baby's face.
5. Offer your baby other shiny things to explore. Look for reflections and sing again.
6. Allow plenty of time for exploring and repetition.

Another idea: Explore some shiny and reflective paper and shiny fabric together.

DID YOU KNOW?

Babies find it easiest to see objects and patterns that have a strong contrast; for example, black on white.

Rock Star
rocking and feeling safe

WHAT YOU NEED:

- a blanket or a square of fleece

Ready for more?

Rock a teddy bear or soft toy from side to side as you sing the rhyme.

If your baby is older, sit him in a large box or plastic crate. Rock it gently from side to side as you sing the song.

WHAT TO DO:

1. Sit on the floor with your knees bent and slightly apart and your feet firmly on the floor. Hold your baby gently facing you, wrapped snugly in a blanket, so that you can easily look into each other's faces.

2. Sing this song to your baby. The tune to "Frère Jacques" fits, but if you like you can choose or make up your own. Keep it slow and steady.

Rock together, rock together,
Here we go, to and fro.
Rocking very gently, rocking very gently
To and fro, here we go.

3. As you sing the rhyme, rock gently together to the song. Start and finish gently.

4. Smile and hold the baby's gaze as you sing and rock.

Another idea: Sing the song while you rock your baby in his stroller.

DID YOU KNOW?

Babies are sensitive to rhythm from their earliest days.

HELPFUL HINTS

If your baby needs extra reassurance, play the game standing up, holding him closely, snuggled in to your shoulder. You can also rock with your baby by simply holding his hands.

What is your baby learning?

This game will lead to the development of balance and to expressing feelings. Watch your baby carefully to see if he is looking, concentrating, showing pleasure, and later, swaying.

See Here
copying facial expressions

- a floppy hat
- a pair of plastic sunglasses

Ready for more?
Help your baby put the hat on her head. Sing the song and then gently tip it off into her lap. Put the hat on a teddy or doll and sing the song, tipping off the hat at the end.

WHAT TO DO:

1. Make sure your baby is sitting comfortably and is well supported. Sit opposite your baby so that your faces are at a similar level.
2. Give your baby the floppy hat to feel. Hold out your hand, and help your baby to pass you the hat.
3. Pop the hat on your head and sing, "Where is my hat? Where is my hat?" to the tune of "Frère Jacques." When baby is looking at you, tip the hat suddenly off your head, and say, "Gone!"
4. Wait to see if your baby looks at or reaches for the hat. Play the game again.
5. Try the same game with the sunglasses.

Another idea: Look out for tinsel wigs and novelty sunglasses from fairs and novelty shops. These are great for encouraging looking.

DID YOU KNOW?
Babies find it easiest to see the colors black and yellow.

HELPFUL HINTS
Your baby may be anxious when your appearance changes. Go slowly, and keep peeping out from under the hat so that she can see it's still you. Help your baby use two hands together.

What is your baby learning?
This game helps to develop attention and encourages first words.

HELPFUL HINTS

Your baby may need you to guide his hands gently to your face or an object. Allow your baby plenty of time to lift his head to look and focus on you.

Reach Out
reaching and touching

WHAT YOU NEED:

- a blanket

Ready for more?

Put a light scarf over your head and let baby pull it off. Stand in front of a mirror and help your baby to reach out for the reflection.

What is your baby learning?

This game will help your baby learn to reach out and take turns. Watch your baby to see if he is looking at, holding, or grasping the object around your neck, and listen for sounds he makes.

WHAT TO DO:

1. Hold your baby securely so he can see your face. Make sure you have his attention.
2. Open your mouth wide, and encourage baby to reach out and touch your face. Praise any movement he makes toward you with his hands or arms.
3. Now lay your baby on his back, on a blanket on the floor.
4. Lean over baby until your face is within reach. Talk to him and encourage him to reach up and touch your face. Remember to give praise and smiles for every effort at reaching, touching, and holding.

Another idea: Hang a small object around your neck and lean over so baby can reach up for it.

DID YOU KNOW?

Young babies can't see very far or judge distances, so be ready to help in the early stages.

Take This
holding and letting go

WHAT YOU NEED:

- a few everyday objects, small and light enough for baby to hold; for example, a small whisk, a little wooden or baby spoon, a plastic lid, a small plastic toy

Ready for more?

Make a treasure basket for your baby to play with. Fill it with interesting objects to explore and hold. Make a 'pat mat' from a small zip lock bag filled with cotton wool, crinkly paper, or even paint.

WHAT TO DO:

1. Make sure your baby is sitting comfortably and is well supported. Sit opposite your baby so that your faces are at a similar level.
2. Hold out one of the objects. Talk to your baby and encourage her to take the object. Hold it close enough for her to be able touch it, but far enough away so she has to reach out.
3. Let your baby play with the object, talking to her about it as she does. Smile and praise her for holding it.
4. Offer another object and praise your baby if she takes it.
5. Allow your baby time to play with the objects and experiment.

Another idea: Use some crinkly paper or textured fabric instead of an object.

What is your baby learning?

This game helps your baby grow and develop the muscles she needs to control her hands and arms (important later when she learns to write).

HELPFUL HINTS

Make sure the objects are light enough for your baby to grip and wave about. Don't rush things. Sit with your baby as she explores the objects, encouraging her and praising her efforts.

Shake It All About!
shaking and rattling

WHAT YOU NEED:

- some things that rattle; for example, wrist rattles, tins containing beads or pasta, baby rattles, bells, boxes, purses with coins, snack tubes with small pebbles, zip lock bags with beads

Ready for more?

Allow plenty of time for listening and for your baby to respond. Give him lots of smiles, and praise his efforts.

Try rattling under a blanket or cloth and see if he can pull the blanket off to get the rattle.

WHAT TO DO:

1. Collect a few rattling objects. Make sure they are light enough for your baby to hold and shake.
2. Sit opposite your baby and pick up one of the rattles. Shake it to attract his attention.
3. Shake the rattle rhythmically, saying, "Look, look, look. Shake, shake, shake."
4. Offer him the rattle, and wait for your baby to respond to it. Give it a little shake to tempt him.
5. Try holding a rattle each and sharing the shaking.

Another idea: Play with bells, maracas, and other simple musical instruments.

What is your baby learning?

In this game, your baby is responding to sound and rhythm. Interacting with you will help him learn to relate to people. Look for grasping, smiling, shaking, and signs of listening.

HELPFUL HINTS

Allow plenty of time for your baby to focus on the rattle and reach out for it. Smile at and praise your baby when he responds to the rattles.

Snuggle Up
feeling close, feeling good

WHAT YOU NEED:

- a soft blanket
- one of your baby's comfort toys
- soothing music and a soft lamp

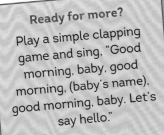

Ready for more?

Play a simple clapping game and sing, "Good morning, baby, good morning, (baby's name), good morning, baby. Let's say hello."

What is your baby learning?

This activity helps to develop your baby's concentration; it will reinforce her bond with you. Watch for her to show pleasure and respond to your attention.

WHAT TO DO:

1. Sit with your baby on your lap, so that she can easily see your face. Remember that she will focus best at 8"-10" away.

2. Place the lamp at eye level where your baby can see it, but not so that it will dazzle her.

3. Give your baby her comfort toy, and help her to hold it in her arms. Gently spread the blanket over both of you.

4. Sing hello to your baby, stroking her cheek softly as you sing her name.

5. Switch on the lamp and the music. Tap the light gently to draw attention to it, and sing: "Hello, (baby's name), hello, (baby's name). Let's look, let's look, let's look."

Another idea: Sit with baby on your knee, facing away from you, holding her comfort toy in front of her. Make the comfort toy dance, and then bring it to the baby for a hug.

DID YOU KNOW?

Babies like to be held tight; it makes them feel secure. But don't squeeze too hard!

HELPFUL HINTS

Make sure your baby's head is well supported. Some babies can't yet regulate their body temperature. Make sure she doesn't get too hot under the blanket.

Say It with Music
rocking and dancing a greeting

WHAT YOU NEED:

- two wrist toys or hair scrunchies

Ready for more?

Sit on the floor with your baby facing you. Hold his shoulders and rock gently from side to side. Chant quietly:

Side to side, here we go, stopping now to say hello.

Stop rocking, say "Hello," and start again.

What is your baby learning?

This activity helps to develop your baby's concentration and will reinforce his bond with you. Watch for him to show pleasure and respond to your attention.

WHAT TO DO:

1. Slip a wrist toy or hair scrunchie over your baby's wrist and put one on your own wrist.
2. Stand up, holding your baby facing you and close to your body.
3. Sway gently and rhythmically, dancing with and smiling at your baby. Hold your baby's hand and gently shake it, singing:

*Good to see you, thanks for coming,
    hello, (baby's name),
Good to see you, thanks for coming,
    hello, (baby's name).*

The song should be lively and bouncy, but be careful you don't shake your baby up and down too much.

Another idea: Change your song. Put on some bouncy music and sing along with your baby.

DID YOU KNOW?

Babies will often respond to music they heard in the womb, such as the theme from your favorite soap opera!

27

Hello, Goodbye
greetings and saying goodbye

WHAT YOU NEED:

- a favorite teddy bear (or other soft toy)
- a blanket
- a toy cot (or cardboard box)

Ready for more?

Give your baby a small blanket to put on the teddy in his bed. Encourage baby to fetch "Special Ted." before saying goodbye and putting it in the cot.

WHAT TO DO:

1. Sit on a blanket on the floor with your baby.
2. Hold the teddy or toy behind your back and slowly bring it around to where baby can see it. Say, "Hello, teddy" (or whatever the toy is called).
3. Play with the teddy and after a little while say, "Bye bye, teddy." Move the teddy around behind your back.
4. Keep this teddy or toy special. Encourage your baby to hug and look after it.

Another idea: When you've finished playing, stroke the teddy together and tell your baby, "Time for teddy to sleep." Together, put the teddy to bed in the cot and cover it up.

DID YOU KNOW?

Young babies have poor vision but learn to recognize their parents' faces very quickly.

What is your baby learning?

This activity will help your baby develop the social skills of greeting and saying goodbye. Most children find that having a special toy gives important feelings of security.

HELPFUL HINTS

A soft, "beanie"-type teddy will be easier for a young baby to hold. Help your baby uncurl his fingers by rubbing gently on the backs of his hands.

Do You Mean Me?
looking, smiling, and responding to her name

WHAT YOU NEED:

- a teddy bear or other favorite soft toy

Ready for more?

Sing the hello song while smiling and waving to your baby in a mirror.

WHAT TO DO:

1. Hold your baby facing you on your knee. Sit so you can look into each other's faces at baby's eye level.
2. Tickle your baby's cheek gently and sing, "Hello, (baby's name), hello, (baby's name), hello, hello, hello."
3. Take one of your baby's hands gently to your face and sing the rhyme again, using your own name in place of your baby's name.
4. Do this a couple of times. Then hold the teddy close and help your baby to hold or pat the teddy. Sing, "Hello, teddy, hello, teddy, hello, hello hello."
5. Give your baby plenty of time, attention, and smiles. Imitate any sounds she makes and encourage her to look at you or the teddy as you sing each part of the rhyme.

Another idea: Vary the pace, or use funny voices and whispers to grab her attention.

DID YOU KNOW?

Newborn babies can't hear well. The middle ear of a newborn is full of fluid. Keep talking!

What is your baby learning?

This activity will help with listening and will encourage attention. It also develops turn taking.

HELPFUL HINTS

To provide an extra reward, use a soft toy that squeaks when you squeeze it. If your baby is younger, make sure her head is well supported.

What is your baby learning?

This activity helps develop listening and understanding, and it is good preparation for your baby's first words.

Again, Again!
asking for more

DID YOU KNOW?

Babies feel security and reassurance when something is repeated.

WHAT YOU NEED:

- a jar of bubble mixture and a bubble wand
- some craft feathers

Ready for more?

Build towers of bricks and knock them down. Let your baby join in. Encourage sounds, words, or gestures to mean "Again" each time the tower is knocked down.
Play a favorite tickle game and then ask your baby, "Again?"

WHAT TO DO:

1. Sit opposite your baby so that your faces are level.
2. Call his name; then, gently blow some bubbles so that they float close. Make sure they don't go into your baby's face.
3. Say, "Pop!" and gently reach up to pop the bubbles. Pause for a moment and wait for your baby to make a sound, reach out, or gesture to request more.
4. Say, "Again?" and wait for a sound, word, or gesture. Repeat, "Again?" and blow some more bubbles. Allow plenty of time for your baby to show you he wants you to do it again.
5. Play the same game with the feathers, blowing them high into the air and waiting for them to float down before asking, "Again?"

Another idea: Play the game with tissue or transparent paper.

Peekaboo
smiles and surprises

WHAT YOU NEED:

- small (roughly 12") squares of fabrics with different textures—net, fur, wool, and so on
- a blanket

Ready for more?

Try hiding noisy toys under the fabric. Can you find them together? Put the blanket over the head of a doll or soft toy. Play peekaboo. Encourage your baby to pull off the cloth when you say, "Boo."

WHAT TO DO:

1. Give your baby time to pat, pull, and explore the fabrics. Experience the sensation of feeling them on your and your baby's cheeks, fingers, and toes.
2. Hold out a hand in a "Give it to me" gesture and say, "Thank you." Gently take the fabric, hold it up to your face, and play peekaboo.
3. Each time you play, let your baby choose the fabric.
4. Spread out the blanket. Hold it up and play peekaboo. Hold it high in the air and encourage your baby to come under the blanket with you. Snuggle up under the blanket and play peekaboo with a corner. Encourage eye contact by rewarding with smiles and lots of attention.

Another idea: Play peekaboo around the edge of a door.

What is your baby learning?

This activity helps develop listening and understanding, and is good preparation for your baby's first words.

Up and Down
lifting up and using the voice

WHAT YOU NEED:

- No special equipment for this activity.

Ready for more?

Babies love this game, and some like to be lifted quite vigorously. Play the game standing up, so the feeling of up and down is greater.

Encourage baby to play the game with a toy.

WHAT TO DO:

1. Hold your baby in your arms or under her arms so you are face to face.
2. Look into your baby's eyes and say, "Hello, (baby's name), hello, (baby's name). Shall we play a game?"
3. Lift your baby gently up and down and say, "Here we go up, up, up. Here we go down, down, down." Use a simple tune or a singsong voice. Smile as you talk.
4. Do this a couple of times.
5. Look at your baby the whole time you are playing this game. Imitate any sounds your baby makes and encourage her to look at you as you sing.

Another idea: Sit your baby in your lap and play the game with a soft toy, lifting it up and down.

DID YOU KNOW?

Touching helps your baby to grow by stimulating growth-promoting hormones.

HELPFUL HINTS

Whisper or use a funny voice to get and keep your baby's attention.
Remember that young babies need their heads supported when you're playing physical games.

What is your baby learning?

This activity helps to develop listening and attending, and promotes the idea of taking turns. See if you can spot your baby turning to the sound and showing anticipation.

What is your baby learning?

This helps to develop copying and making sounds, and it encourages taking turns.

Echo, Echo
copying sounds and expressions

DID YOU KNOW?

Babies have a natural tendency to copy. Learning to copy is essential to early learning.

WHAT YOU NEED:

- No special equipment for this activity.

Ready for more?

With older babies make the expressions more complicated.
Play the game in a mirror so that your baby can see himself, as well as you.

WHAT TO DO:

1. Sit with your baby in your lap, so your faces are level. If your baby is very young, keep your face close (about 8"-10" is best).
2. Call your baby's name or talk to him to get his attention.
3. Use exaggerated expressions and a lively voice to maintain his interest.
4. Now use different facial expressions and sounds to encourage your baby to watch and copy you. Try slowly poking your tongue out, opening your mouth wide, popping your lips, blowing out your cheeks, and so on.
5. Be patient. Small babies have to work hard at copying you—their muscles are immature. Praise any response!

Another idea: Play this game at changing time.

Babbling
exchanging sounds and noises

WHAT YOU NEED:

- No special equipment for this activity.

Ready for more?

Older babies and children love echo games. Try some simple "My turn, your turn" songs or rhymes. Try passing an object as you make the sound; for example, a small soft toy or rattle.

What is your baby learning?

This game helps your baby develop concentration and taking turns, and it leads to first words. Watch your baby to see her copying, using her voice, and watching you.

WHAT TO DO:

1. Sit with your baby in your lap facing you, close enough to see your face.
2. Call baby's name to attract her attention.
3. When you have her attention, make a short repetitive sound—*goo-goo, ma-ma, da-da, la-la, na-na,* and so on.
4. Wait for your baby to respond. If she doesn't, make the sound again and wait for a response. Praise any response she makes, even if it isn't the same sound as you made (it probably won't be).
5. Keep going, taking turns and exchanging smiles as well as sounds.
6. Stop when your baby loses concentration or interest.

Another idea: Let your baby start the exchange and copy sounds she makes.

DID YOU KNOW?

Babies communicate physically before they can communicate verbally, and they quickly learn key gestures.

HELPFUL HINTS

If your baby is still very young, remember to stay close. She won't see you properly if you're more than about 10" away. Give your baby plenty of time to respond—it may take several tries for her to get the idea.

What is your baby learning?

This helps to develop attention and listening skills and promotes turn-taking. Watch for your baby looking, listening, responding, and copying actions.

Copy Cat
copying facial expressions

WHAT YOU NEED:

- a few moments of one-to-one quiet time
- a comfortable place to sit with your baby

Ready for more?

Sing rhymes and songs to your baby, tapping the rhythm gently on his stomach or back.
Play anticipation games, such as, "I'm coming to tickle you."

WHAT TO DO:

1. Hold your baby and support his head so that you can easily look into his face.
2. Remember that young babies focus best around 10" away. Make sure you are close enough for your baby to be able to see you clearly.
3. Sing hello to your baby. Stroke his cheeks, and gently engage his attention. Pause; then, stick out your tongue. Repeat this every 20 seconds or so. Keep going for about two minutes to give your baby plenty of time to respond by copying your action.
4. Reward any response by smiling and praising.

Another idea: Try some different actions, such as twitching your nose, smiling, and so on. Repeat the action for one to two minutes to give your baby plenty of time to copy.

DID YOU KNOW?

The more stimulating experiences you can give your baby, the more brain power is built for future learning.

Fingers and Toes
fun with finger puppets

WHAT YOU NEED:

- some fur fabric (bright green would be good, but any color will do)
- fabric glue or a simple sewing kit
- scissors

Ready for more?

Put your baby's hands between your own and rub them gently, singing, "Rub-a-dub dub, rub-a-dub dub."

Lay your baby on her back, hold her ankles in the air, and play peekaboo between her feet.

What is your baby learning?

This helps to develop attention, listening skills, and understanding. It leads to babbling, and from that to first words.

WHAT TO DO:

1. Make a very simple green caterpillar finger puppet to fit your index finger. Use fabric glue or stitches to fix the sides.

2. Make sure that your baby is well supported, perhaps sitting sideways on your knee so that you can look into each other's eyes.

3. Try this new finger rhyme, gradually wriggling and creeping the finger puppet up baby's arm into the palm of her hand, around and around; then, down her arm, tummy, and legs, to her toes:

Wriggle, wriggle, here I come.
Caterpillar on my thumb.
Round and round, off he goes.
All the way down to my toes.

Another idea: Start the rhyme very slowly, and pause before running your fingers down to baby's toes for a gentle tickle.

DID YOU KNOW?

Your baby's index fingers are more sensitive than any of the others. Encourage using them to touch and explore.

HELPFUL HINTS

Some children may prefer a gentle pressure to a very light touch. Try both and watch baby to see what she likes best. Stopping in the middle of a rhyme, with an exaggerated pause and gasp, is a great attention grabber.

HELPFUL HINTS

You can be livelier with older children, but for small babies go gently and make sure they have good enough head control before you play this sort of game. Most babies love this game, but if your baby doesn't, stop at once, and don't worry. He simply might not be ready for it yet.

Almost Ballroom
moving to a rhythm

WHAT YOU NEED:

- No special equipment for this activity.

DID YOU KNOW?

Most babies enjoy music, and it can develop brain power.

Ready for more?

Get an older child or your partner to sit on the floor opposite you. Pat a beach ball or balloon between you. Find a hat and take it in turns putting it on the baby and taking it off; then, do the same thing, but on yourself instead of the baby. This is another game where it's good to have an older child or a partner to join in.

WHAT TO DO:

1. Hold your baby comfortably in your arms, facing you.
2. Move around in a circle, taking side steps and singing:

   Step and step, 1, 2, 3, step and step, dance with me,
   Step and step, 1, 2, 3, step and stop, look at me!

3. On the last line, stop suddenly and swing your baby smoothly high in the air and hold him there. Hold his eye contact for a moment before lowering him gently down again and continuing the dance.

Another idea:

If you have a friend who also has a baby, it's great fun to get them to join in. The babies will enjoy being together and watching each other.

What is your baby learning?

This game helps anticipation, the enjoyment of repetition, and concentration. Watch your baby to see if he is feeling the rhythm and moving with you, sharing fun, and showing trust and anticipation.

DID YOU KNOW?

Newborn babies cry, but they don't produce any tears. Tears don't start until 3–12 weeks.

Eye to Eye
singing and rocking

WHAT YOU NEED:

- a few moments of one-to-one quiet time
- a comfortable place to sit with your baby

WHAT TO DO:

1. Every baby needs the opportunity for quiet conversations, and this game is to encourage them.
2. Hold your baby with her head well supported so that you can look at her face easily and she can see you.
3. Remember that young babies focus best at around 10" away. Make sure you are close enough for your baby to be able to see you clearly.
4. Sing a simple nursery rhyme or song as you gently rock backward and forward. Take it slowly—remember, babies need time to focus and follow.
5. Talk quietly to your baby as you rock. Encourage and praise her as she moves her face, hands, and body.

Another idea: Look, smile, and wait for the baby to smile back. Praise her. Try again, smile again, praise again.

Ready for more?

Each time you change or feed your baby, talk to her and make eye contact. Sing lots of rhymes and songs to your baby, looking at her as you sing.

HELPFUL HINTS

When deciding where to sit, choose a spot where the light is falling on your face so your baby can see you easily. Some children find the rocking soothing; others will respond better if you keep still. Try both and see which your baby prefers.

What is your baby learning?

This activity develops attention and listening skills and encourages responding and taking turns. It is good preparation for learning to converse.

Here Comes Teddy
hide-and-seek fun

WHAT YOU NEED:

- a small teddy bear or soft toy

Ready for more?

Play other simple games of anticipation, such as, Peekaboo or I'm Coming to Tickle You! Play these "wait for it" games at changing time.

WHAT TO DO:

1. This game is about listening and anticipation, and taking meaning from the tone of your voice.
2. Prop your baby securely in a baby chair or on a cushion. If your baby is very young, make sure he has good head support.
3. Kneel or sit facing baby, so he can see your face and what you are doing.
4. Using a lively and enthusiastic tone say:

   Here comes teddy (or rabbit or whatever),
   here he comes,
   Along your legs and up to your tum!

5. Walk the toy up the baby's legs and tummy as you talk.
6. Praise any response and indication of "again."

Another idea: Make the toy appear from different places, such as behind you, behind baby, or from under a blanket.

HELPFUL HINTS

An expressive voice and slightly higher tone will attract your baby's attention and engage him in the game. Show your baby the toy before you start the game, so he knows what to expect. Sometimes stop in the middle of a song, pause, and gasp to grab his attention.

What is your baby learning?

This game develops attention, listening skills and understanding, and stimulates first words. Watch your baby to see if he is watching, responding (gurgling, looking excited, waving limbs), and showing anticipation.

Which One?
it's your choice

WHAT YOU NEED:

- a warm, comfortable, familiar place
- a basket of small toys and other objects, easy for your baby to hold

Ready for more?

Offer your baby choices as soon as she can hold something. Try finger foods, pieces of fabric, or small soft toys. Whenever you are with your baby, talk about what you are doing. Continue, even if she doesn't respond.

WHAT TO DO:

1. Sit opposite your baby. Make sure that she is supported.
2. Pick up two of the toys or objects, and hold them where she can reach out for them. Say in a singsong voice:

   Which one would you like to have?
   Take the one you'd like to have.

3. Watch for a response to one or the other, and encourage your baby to take the toy in her hand. Name the objects as you offer them. Talk aloud to her about what you are doing.
4. Let your baby play with the object for a while before holding out two more objects. Praise her when she reaches for an object and holds it.

Another idea: Play the game with objects that make a sound or are brightly colored.

What is your baby learning?

This activity is good preparation for learning to name things, and will help to lay the groundwork for conversations.

Angel's Delight
messy play on reflective surfaces

WHAT YOU NEED:

- a safety mirror, a large shiny metal tray, or a tin lid
- pudding or thick yogurt
- a can of whipped cream

Ready for more?

Draw circles and lines in the pudding. Tape bubble wrap to a table top so that it covers it. Spread the pudding and whipped-cream mixture over the bubble wrap and explore how it feels.

WHAT TO DO:

1. Spoon some pudding on the mirror, tray, or tin lid.
2. Sit beside your baby and play together, patting and poking the pudding. Encourage your baby to trail her fingers through the pudding, squeezing.
3. Add some whipped cream, and encourage your baby to use two hands to mix the whipped cream and pudding together.
4. Give a simple commentary on what she is doing, using single words and short phrases. Comment on changes, such as *more, all gone,* or *stirring.* Encourage new actions.

Another idea: Add plastic scrubbers and dishwashing brushes. Encourage exploration of *up* and *down,* as well as circular movements.

HELPFUL HINTS

Try this activity using the pudding straight from the fridge for a very different sensory experience from using it at room temperature. Some babies don't like getting their hands messy. If your baby is one of these, offer her clean brushes, rollers, and spoons to stir the mixtures.

What is your baby learning?

This encourages exploration and investigation, and it starts to develop the movement and control your baby needs for writing.

Find out which textures your baby seems to like and talk about these. Allow him plenty of time to explore. **SAFETY NOTE:** Do not leave small babies alone with strings. They could become entangled in them.

Lay It on the Line
a line of things to feel

WHAT YOU NEED:

- lots of different surfaces and textures: pieces of fabric, corrugated cardboard, bubble wrap, a glove, some big beads or buttons, and so on
- string or yarn
- a washing line or cord

Ready for more?

Make a portable toy by threading moving pieces on a shoe or boot lace. Try a line of things that make sounds, such as bells, shells, rattles, or small toys.

What is your baby learning?

This activity helps with the foundations for investigating and exploring, as well as describing things.

WHAT TO DO:

1. Sit your baby in a seat or prop him up with a cushion where he can easily see you.
2. Tie a piece of washing line or cord between two chairs. Using small bits of string or yarn, attach some of the things you have collected to the line or string items along the line.
3. Talk about what you are doing as you do it, and name the things you are tying or stringing on the line.
4. When you have about six different things fixed on the line, move your baby to where he can reach it.
5. Encourage him to reach out for and grasp the things on the line. Talk and listen.

Another idea: Attach several strings to a washing line or cord and fix it above the changing table.

DID YOU KNOW?

Although babies have a good sense of smell, few have much of a sense of taste—though most prefer sweet tastes.

HELPFUL HINTS

Your baby might need you to move her hands gently to the objects. If your baby clenches her fists, gently tickle the back of her hands to help her open them up.

What is your baby learning?

This activity helps with making choices, reaching, and investigating.

Spots or Stripes
exploring pattern and texture

WHAT YOU NEED:

- a collection of everyday objects with spots, stripes, slots, and holes (for example, a tea strainer, draining spoon, spaghetti measurer, cookie cutters, or a striped towel)
- a tray

Ready for more?

Try cutting holes and slits in old pieces of fabric to poke hands through. Explore hair scrunchies, bangles, and bracelets together. Make a collection of cardboard and plastic tubes to explore.

WHAT TO DO:

1. Clear a space and remove any objects that might be distracting.
2. Make sure your baby is sitting in a well-supported position.
3. Offer her one of the objects from your collection. Encourage reaching, grasping, and holding with two hands.
4. Explore the object together. Hold it up and look at it. Let your baby handle it. Try gently touching her hands or feet with it. Feel the holes, peep through the slots, and touch the spots. Talk all the time, naming the object and telling your baby about it. Don't worry that she won't understand you—it's the act of communicating and describing that's important.
5. Change to a new thing when you judge that your baby is ready to move on. Allow plenty of time for her to explore the tray of objects without interruption. Stay with your baby while she explores.

DID YOU KNOW?

Babies can make out colors from about 2 weeks. They prefer strong colors and bigger patterns.

Squeeze and Poke
making changes

WHAT YOU NEED:

- small quantities of cooked sticky rice, mashed potatoes, and flavored gelatin
- small plastic bowls and cups
- small plastic trays, plastic lids, and so on

Ready for more?

Make small, sticky rice balls and hold them out so your baby can reach for and grasp them. Provide a slotted spoon or plastic potato masher so that baby can pound, mix, and poke.

WHAT TO DO:

1. Make sure that your baby is sitting well supported in a baby chair and dressed (or undressed!), ready for messy play.
2. Sit opposite your baby and place a small quantity of sticky rice on his tray. Pat it, poke it, and gently squeeze some through your own fingers. Encourage him to feel it.
3. Help your baby to squeeze it, poke it, and so on. Cup your hand for him to poke the rice.
4. Give plenty of uninterrupted time and attention. Encourage your baby to pat and rub the rice with both hands.
5. Do the same with the mashed potatoes, and then with the flavored gelatin. You could mix them all together for a very messy medley!

Another idea: Try some very soft bread dough as an alternative.

DID YOU KNOW

All newborn babies have pug noses. The bridge of the nose isn't there at birth—it grows later.

HELPFUL HINTS

Your baby may be wary of such new textures. Don't worry if he is—just introduce them slowly. Give your baby as much time as he needs—he may prefer to watch you first.

What is your baby learning?

This activity helps develops fine motor control and leads to understanding cause and effect.

What is your baby learning?

This leads to exploring and to understanding cause and effect.

The String's the Thing
fun with strings and ribbons

WHAT YOU NEED:

- ribbons (several different colors if possible)
- scissors
- plastic bangles
- small shakers, bells, and rattles

Ready for more?

Use different textures and types of string and ribbon attached to different sound makers. Fix a plastic spoon to a ribbon as an alternative type of handle.

WHAT TO DO:

1. Cut several pieces of ribbon, each about 6"–8" long.
2. Tie a plastic bangle to each cut length of ribbon. Tie a rattle, shaker or bell(s) to the other end of each ribbon. Check that each one is secure.
3. Sit your baby in a well-supported position.
4. Place one of the shakers on the floor or on a tray in front of your baby. Offer her the bangle to hold. Help her to grasp it if she needs you to.
5. Talk and sing to your baby as she explores the bangle. Gently tug the ribbon and shaker toward her, and encourage her to try to pull it. Reward any attempt to pull by smiling and saying, "Again?"

Another idea: Put the items on a tin tray. The items will make a satisfying noise for your baby as she pulls and drops them.

DID YOU KNOW?

Babies often need background noise to help them get to sleep—the womb is not a quiet place!

All Steamed Up!
first marks

WHAT YOU NEED:

- a mirror or window

Ready for more?

Use a small hand mirror for the same game. Play the game at changing or bath time.

WHAT TO DO:

1. Hold your baby in your arms and stand very near the window or mirror, so you can both see. Talk to him all the time as you look at each other in the mirror.
2. Gently breathe on the window or mirror, so a small patch of the glass mists up. Say, "Look, all gone!" as your faces disappear.
3. Make sure that your baby is looking at the misty mirror. Now clear the small patch away with your hand.
4. Greet your baby in the mirror again.
5. Now breathe on a different part of the mirror or window and draw a smiling face in the mist

Another idea: Get up really close and let your baby pat the mirror so he makes marks, too.

DID YOU KNOW?

Reading to your baby increases sensitivity to the sounds of language and helps bonding.

HELPFUL HINTS

Try to reduce distractions behind you which could be reflected in mirrors or windows. Try to avoid having light behind you. Your baby will see you better if the light is shining on your faces.

What is your baby learning?

This activity helps your baby to learn to use fingers and hands to investigate and make marks. It also helps your baby begin to understand object permanence.

Hold It
touching and exploring

WHAT YOU NEED:

- pieces of gift ribbon, string, or cord
- small and interesting objects such as beads, small bells, and so on

Ready for more?

Make a simple mobile and hang it where your baby can see it when she is lying down. Hang old CDs in trees and bushes in your garden or on a balcony, where your baby can watch them spinning and shining.

WHAT TO DO:

1. Cut some lengths of string or ribbon, and tie one of the objects securely on the end of each.
2. Sit your baby facing you in a chair or securely supported on a rug or mat.
3. Choose one of the strings and dangle the object in front of baby, just within reach of her outstretched arms but not too close.
4. Keep the object as still as you can, so your baby can focus on it.
5. Talk to your baby and encourage her to reach out for the object. Lower the string so she can pull the object towards her. Do not leave the baby unattended with the string.
6. Try again with a different object.

Another idea: Hang strings above the changing area. Change the objects every few days.

DID YOU KNOW?

Babies can grab things and hang on to them tightly, but often need help to let go again!

HELPFUL HINTS

A pillow or cushion on each side of a young baby may help her to lie still and concentrate. Brightly colored objects and things that make sounds will add interest and help your baby stay interested.

What is your baby learning?

This activity helps your baby to practice focusing her eyes and leads to grabbing and holding, which in turn develops hand control.

Reach for It
black-and-white patterns

WHAT YOU NEED:

- white card
- black card (or paper)
- scissors, glue, and ribbon
- a hoop or baby gym

Ready for more?

Cut out eyes, noses, and mouths to make black-and-white face patterns. Add shiny borders to the cards.

WHAT TO DO:

1. Cut some different shapes from the black card. Try zigzags, circles, triangles, squares, blobs.
2. Glue them to the white card to make black-and-white contrasting patterns. Make different patterns on each side of the white card.
3. Tie the cards securely to the hoop or baby gym. Lay your baby under the baby gym or hang the hoop securely over his cot so that the cards are within easy reach.
4. Tap the cards and encourage your baby to look at them, to reach out to them, and to pat them.

Another idea: Try a chess-board pattern.

DID YOU KNOW?

Contrasting patterns help babies learn to focus. They like checker boards and spotty fabrics.

HELPFUL HINTS

Tape some small bells to the back of the card. Shake the card gently to help baby focus and look in the direction of the sound. Try this with your baby in a bouncy seat or car seat—hang the cards from a string slung between two dining chairs.

What is your baby learning?

Through this activity, your baby will strengthen her eye muscles; she will also develop the muscle coordination she needs to grab and hold.

Roll up two small towels and place one on each side of a small baby to give him extra support and comfort. Experiment by holding the mobiles in different positions to see where your baby can most easily focus.

What is your baby learning?

This activity will help your baby learn to follow things with his eyes, as well as develop his attention span. It is a good starter for sensory play.

Look Up
soothing sights

DID YOU KNOW?

Babies are attracted to moving objects. That's why they may often stare at the television.

WHAT YOU NEED:

- some simple mobiles: black-and-white or reflective (if you don't have any, it's easy to make one by hanging objects from a plastic coat hanger)
- a rug for your baby to lie on and a nest of cushions

Ready for more?

Use glitter sticks or bubble tubes to encourage looking and reaching. Shine a flashlight onto a wall for your baby to follow the beam (sit beside him so you don't accidentally shine it into his eyes).

WHAT TO DO:

1. Make sure that your baby is warm and comfortable as he lies on the rug. Enclose the space with cushions.
2. Hang the mobiles above your baby, so he can gaze and focus on them.
3. The mobiles should be close enough for your baby to be able to see them clearly (remember that young babies focus best around 10"). Check that the mobiles are fixed securely to ensure that if your baby pats them, he will not become entangled.
4. Move the mobiles gently and talk to your baby, getting him to look toward the mobiles. Hum a gentle tune, encouraging baby to track the mobile from side to side.

Another idea: Put your baby on his tummy and roll brightly colored or noisy toys from side to side for him to focus on.

Pumpkin Pie
truly messy play!

WHAT YOU NEED:

- a pumpkin
- a sharp knife and chopping board
- a pot and a stove
- a potato masher, milk

Ready for more?

Try gently isolating your baby's index fingers and poking them deep into the mash. Pour a little water over the mash and explore the changing textures. Add a small wooden spoon to bash the mashed pumpkin!

WHAT TO DO:

1. Peel the pumpkin carefully and chop it into even-sized chunks. Boil it for 25 minutes, then drain. Add some cold milk and mash to a smooth consistency. Leave until cool.
2. Make sure your baby is sitting well supported in a chair or on your knee. Take some of the mashed pumpkin and squeeze it through your fingers. Give your baby the chance to smell and feel the texture.
3. Encourage your baby to touch your hands and pat at the mashed pumpkin. Hold her hands gently in yours, and if she is enjoying the experience, rub your hands together gently, exploring the texture of the mashed pumpkin.

Another idea: Place the mashed pumpkin in the fridge for a few hours and play with it again. This will give it a very different sensation.

HELPFUL HINTS

Most babies will put the mashed pumpkin into their mouths. Play this game after a meal when your baby is not hungry.

What is your baby learning?

As well as being great fun, this helps lay the foundation for creativity, develops concentration and investigation, and leads to sensory play.

Shiver and Shake!
exploring vibration

WHAT YOU NEED:

- massage rollers
- toys that shake or vibrate
- a blown-up balloon
- a drum or tambourine

Ready for more?

Try the vibrating toys and massage rollers on legs, feet, and toes. Support your baby on top of a large exercise ball or exer-saucer. Lightly tap the sides of the ball and feel the vibrations.

WHAT TO DO:

1. Sit with your baby well supported, so you can gaze easily into each other's faces. Gently tap your baby's hands and lower arms with your fingertips. Sing, "Tap, tap, tap"—pause—"Tap, tap, tap"—stop.
2. Next give him the massage roller to feel. Help him hold it in both hands and feel it on his fingertips, palms, and the backs of his hands. Very gently, roll it up your baby's forearms.
3. Watch carefully to see how your baby responds to the unfamiliar sensations.
4. Try touching the vibrating toys and tapping the balloon together, or put your baby's hands on the drum or tambourine as you tap the edges to make it vibrate.

Another idea: Fix ribbons tightly across a tray top. Pluck the ribbons.

What is your baby learning?

Exploring vibrations helps lay the foundation for creativity and leads to shared fun and sensory play.

Bubble Trouble
something in the air

WHAT YOU NEED:

- bubbles and a bubble wand

Ready for more?

Put some very bubbly dishwashing-liquid foam on a tray and encourage your baby to pat and feel it. Fill a small fabric or plastic bag with crinkly paper and cooked pasta or rice. Make sure the bag is sealed properly.

WHAT TO DO:

1. Make sure that your baby is sitting or propped in a well-supported position, near a flat surface—for example, a changing table, a wall, a low table, a tray, or a baby chair with a table.
2. Sit opposite your baby and gently blow some bubbles towards him, being careful not to blow them in her face.
3. Try to blow the bubbles near her hands, so she can feel them pop, as well as touch and reach for them.
4. Now blow some bubbles so they land on the flat surface. Put your hand out and pat or poke some of the bubbles. Encourage your baby to reach out and pat the bubbles as they land, too.

Another idea: Try blowing bubbles at changing time. Your baby will love the feeling of them landing and bursting on her stomach.

HELPFUL HINTS

Blow the bubbles in a bright or directed light so the rainbow colors show up. If your baby doesn't like the feel of bubbles on her face or hands, don't worry. Leave it for a while and try again later, but don't persist if there's still a problem.

What is your baby learning?

This activity will help your baby work her fingers and use them to investigate. It also helps to develop concentration.

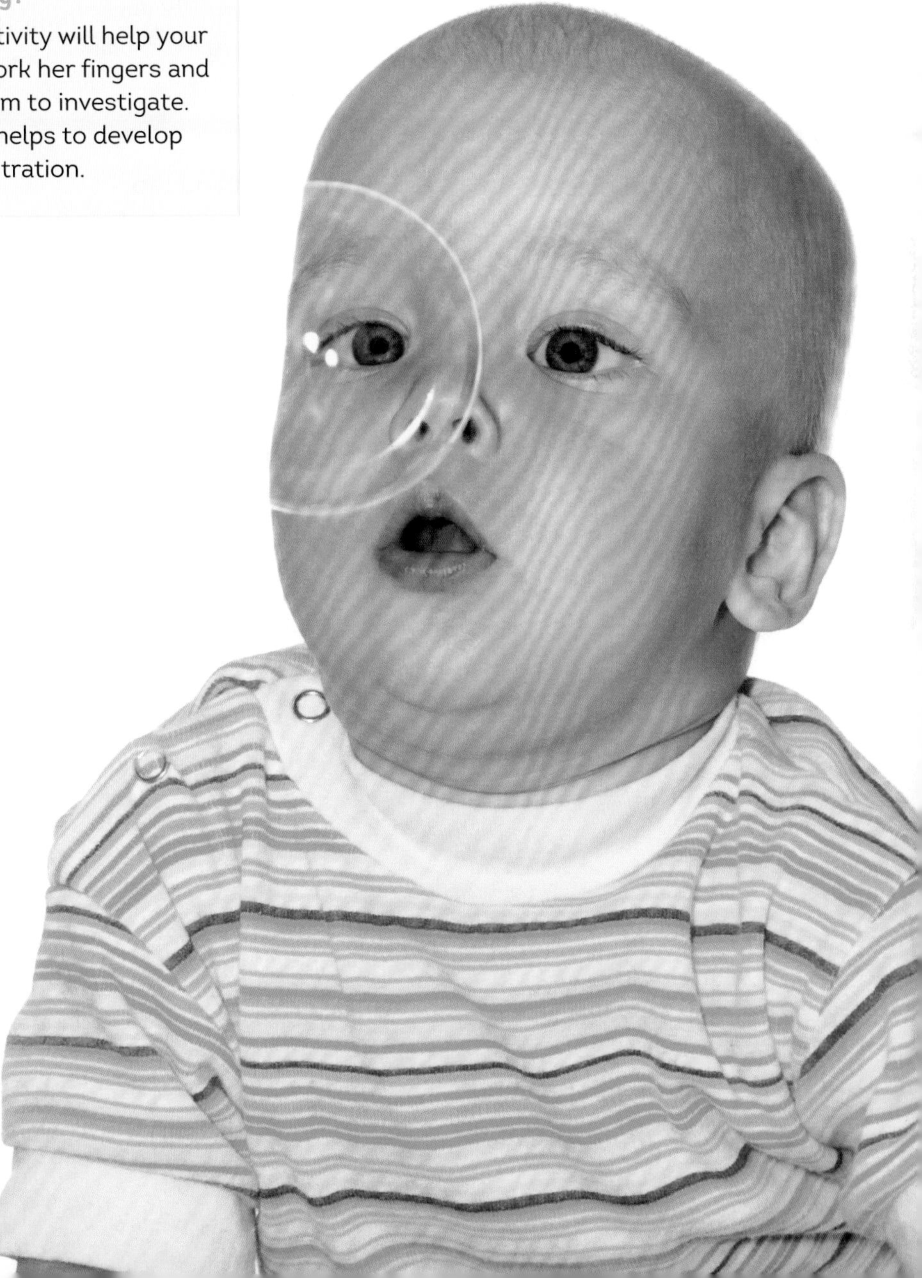

Feel the Difference
texture and treasure

WHAT YOU NEED:

- a shallow plastic tray
- a selection of objects with a range of textures—crinkly paper, a wool sock, furry glove, toothbrush, hard plastic cup, and so on

Ready for more?

Put together a tray of wooden objects with different textures to pat. Offer the objects one at a time for your baby to grasp and hold.

WHAT TO DO:

1. Make a treasure tray by placing some of the objects on the tray (not too many).
2. Pick up one object and tap it on the tray to get your baby's attention.
3. Talk and sing to your baby. Help him to explore the objects.
4. Try rubbing the different textures firmly but gently on the backs of his hands.
5. Encourage your baby to reach for and pat the objects with two hands.
6. Reward his efforts at reaching with words of praise, cuddles, gentle strokes, and tickles.

Another idea: Try patting warm, damp, bubbly sponges.

DID YOU KNOW?

Grasping and holding are reflexes. Babies hang on to things instinctively but have to learn to let go.

HELPFUL HINTS

Make sure that your baby is well supported. It is hard to reach and pat objects if you are still working on your sitting balance! If the highchair is too wide for your baby, you can use a small cushion or rolled up towel next to him to help hold him steady.

What is your baby learning?

This activity helps to develop the coordination and muscles needed for grasping, holding, shaking, and letting go.

What is your baby learning?

This activity helps develop the notion of cause and effect and supports the development of fine motor control.

Grab That
sticks and shakers

DID YOU KNOW?

Babies get some protection from infection from their mothers. This is increased by breastfeeding.

WHAT YOU NEED:

- rattles
- shakers (use purchased ones, or make your own with dried beans, beads, rice, and so on)
- small wooden spoons
- ribbons

Ready for more?

Hold the shakers on alternate sides so your baby can practice reaching to the side. Provide a plastic bowl full of ribbons or scarves to reach for, grab, and explore.

WHAT TO DO:

1. Sit opposite your baby and hold the rattle out so she can reach for it. Hold it in the midline of her vision so she can see it easily.
2. Shake the rattle, call her name, and gently lift her arm from the elbow toward the rattle or shaker. Help her grasp the rattle and shake it. Share her enjoyment of the sound.
3. Tie the ribbons together in a bundle. Trail them through your baby's outstretched hands. Encourage her to grasp the ribbons, or gently twine the ribbons over both of her hands.
4. Offer your baby the wooden spoon to grab and hold. Hold the spoon with her and sing, "Shake, shake, shake; tap, tap, tap."

Another idea: Scarves are great for reaching and grabbing.

Now You See Me
disappearing and reappearing

WHAT YOU NEED:

- a cover—for example, a cloth, towel, blanket or sheet

WHAT TO DO:

1. You can play this game in many places—on the changing table or mat, in a baby chair, during feeding, or when you are having a quiet cuddle.
2. Call your baby's name softly to attract his attention.
3. Hold the cover in front of your face and slowly draw it down so your face appears. Don't move too quickly with a young baby, or he won't be able to follow what is happening. As your face appears, smile and speak gently.
4. Very young babies may not like the "Boo" bit to start with, so make sure you respond to his reactions and take it gently.

Another idea: Let your baby surprise you by putting the cover very gently over his face and letting him pull it off.

DID YOU KNOW?

It takes young babies a long time to understand that things are still there when they can't see them.

Ready for more?

As they get used to this game, most babies enjoy the predicted surprise of "Boo" as you reappear. Try putting the cover right over your head and letting your baby pull it off.

HELPFUL HINTS

Some babies need you to start by covering your face only as far as your eyes, so they are sure you are still there. When your baby is in his stroller, push him gently away from you, then pull him back towards you with a "Boo!"

What is your baby learning?

This activity helps to develop the notion of object permenence and stimulates remembering. It also encourages joining in.

What is your baby learning?

Getting your baby to respond to you and you responding to her is preparation for the give and take of daily life, including learning to take part in conversations.

Look at Me!
a face-to-face game

WHAT YOU NEED:

- No special equipment for this activity.

WHAT TO DO:

1. Sit your baby in a chair or against a secure and comfortable prop.
2. Sit yourself opposite your baby.
3. Call your baby's name to attract her attention
4. Sing or chant to your baby, "Here I am, here I am, close to you. There you are, there you are, close to me." You could use the tune of "Tommy Thumb" or make up your own.
5. As you sing, stroke your baby's hand or arm.
6. Sing the words again. You want your baby to respond, so praise any reaction (such as kicking, waving, smiling) by smiling and saying, "Well done, (baby's name), you are looking at me."

Another idea: Sing the song holding your baby beside you and facing a mirror so you can both see each other and yourselves.

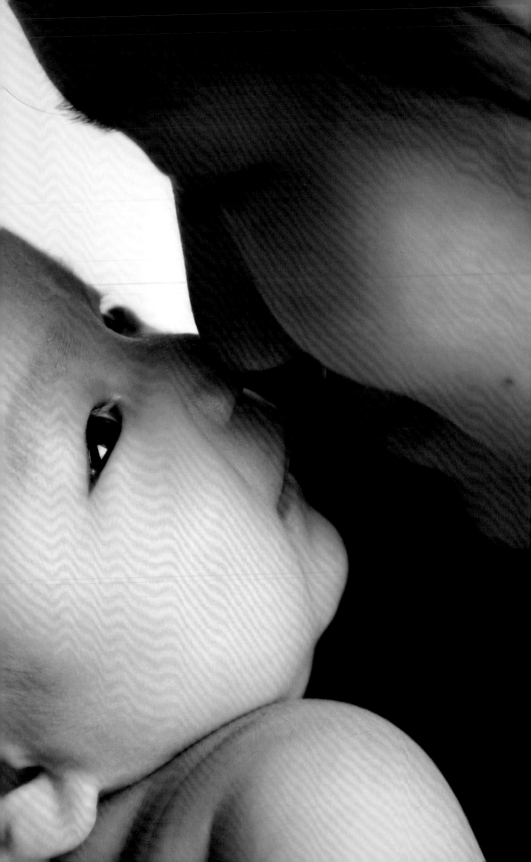

There's Nothing like Cuddling
feeling safe

WHAT YOU NEED:

- a fleece or baby blanket
- a soft toy or teddy bear (optional)

Ready for more?

Sit on a beanbag or floor cushion or in a soft chair with your baby (and an older brother or sister if you can), just watching his world and talking quietly about what you see. This will build his confidence in the safety and security of what goes on around him.

WHAT TO DO:

1. Hold your baby in your lap or your arms.
2. Wrap the fleece or blanket around both of you, so you are together inside the warmth. Include the teddy bear or soft toy if you wish.
3. Hum or talk gently to your baby, repeating his name and singing lullaby songs so he feels safe.
4. Stroke his arms, hands, and back. Use sounds like "shhh," "lala," "mmm," and slow, gentle speech.
5. Rocking gently will increase your baby's feeling of security. Try not to fall asleep yourself!

Another idea: You could walk slowly around your home with your baby in the blanket, talking in a soft voice about what you see.

DID YOU KNOW?

Your baby is very sensitive to how you feel; he will pick up feelings of stress from you. If you relax, it will help him relax, too.

HELPFUL HINTS

Try to spend a little time each day just holding and talking to your baby. Relax and enjoy this cuddling at the end of the day. Stroking soft or furry fabrics can be very relaxing, but small babies will need help with this.

What is your baby learning?

This activity will help to develop confidence, calmness, and the ability to relax.

73

Happy Hands
hands together and to the face

DID YOU **KNOW?**

Learning to clap is an important step in developing physical coordination.

WHAT YOU NEED:

- a wrist toy or elastic hair scrunchie

Ready for more?

Put the wrist toy or bells on your baby's ankle and play again, singing "Happy Feet." As your baby develops, introduce some clapping games to encourage her to bring her hands together and clap.

What is your baby learning?

This will help your baby learn to clap, pat, and reach.

HELPFUL HINTS

Wrist toys are useful for encouraging young babies to lie still at changing time. Vary the pace of the song or use a funny voice to grab your baby's attention.

WHAT TO DO:

1. Sit opposite your baby or with her on your knee, or if your baby is very young, put her on her back on a soft rug. If she is a wriggler, place a rolled up blanket on either side so she can focus on her hands rather than her escape!
2. Gently bring your baby's hands together in the midline and sing:

   Happy hands, happy hands
   Touch it, feel it, happy hands

   You can use the tune of "Jack and Jill," or you can make one up.
3. Tap your baby's hands together gently. Encourage her to feel and shake the wrist toy. Give her plenty of time for unhurried and uninterrupted exploration.
4. Sing the song again, this time gently helping your baby bring her hands together in the midline, and then up to her face so that she can gaze at her hands.

Another idea: Make up some more songs for simple hand games.

What is your baby learning?

Exploration is the theme of this activity, which helps children find out about objects, the materials they're made of, and how they behave.

Pat the Mat
fun with pat mats

DID YOU KNOW?

Touch is important for learning. Children will often pat or slap things to explore them.

WHAT YOU NEED:

- black-and-white fabric
- stick-on Velcro or a simple sewing kit
- scraps of crunchy or crinkly paper for filling

Ready for more?

For an older or more mobile baby, make a giant stamping mat with just a little filling. Noisy toys, bells, and squeakers in the bag will keep the fun going.

WHAT TO DO:

1. Make a simple bag shape, using the Velcro or sewing straight seams for the edges. Fill the bag with scraps of crunchy or crinkly paper. Seal it securely with Velcro or by stitching it.
2. Put the mat on a flat surface, and encourage your baby to pat the mat, using his hands together. Talk and sing as your baby pats the mat.
3. Copy your baby's actions and say or chant, "Pat, pat, pat." Vary your voice to get and keep your baby's attention.
4. Try big, slow movements alternated with quick, tiny pats.

Another idea: Fill the bag with soft sponge or feathers. Add some squeakers for new appeal.

Feeling Good
baby massage

WHAT YOU NEED:

- baby oil (apricot and avocado are both good)
- a changing mat
- a towel, blanket, or shawl

DID YOU KNOW?

There is a biological connection between stroking/massaging a baby and her rate of growth.

Ready for more?
Try back or stomach massages, with gentle, soothing stroking and smoothing. Try the massage as your baby is going to sleep at rest time, to help her relax.

WHAT TO DO:

1. Choose a warm, quiet, draft-free place for this activity. You can rest your baby on your lap or on a changing mat.
2. Sit on the carpet or a cushion, with your back supported by a wall. Put a warm towel on your lap or on the changing mat, and gently lay your baby on the towel.
3. Remove her shoes and any clothing on arms or legs.
4. Pour a little warmed oil on your hands and rub them together, talking to your baby all the time, maintaining eye contact, and telling her in a quiet voice what you are doing.
5. Now gently massage your baby's feet, legs, arms, and hands, rubbing in the oil and talking to her or singing softly.
6. Use the towel to remove any excess oil when you finish.

Another idea: Try some restful music in the background. Calm, classical music works well (look out for compilations with titles like *Tranquility, Relaxation,* or similar).

HELPFUL HINTS

Keep eye contact all the time, and stop if your baby becomes anxious or wriggly. Take care when picking baby up after massage—oily babies are slippery!

What is your baby learning?

As well as stimulating growth, massaging your baby is important for bonding and leads to confidence and trust.

Swing Time
rocking and rolling

WHAT YOU NEED:

- a strong, soft blanket
- a soft mat, rug, or mattress
- a partner or friend to join in

Ready for more?

Move around in a circle as you swing. Try "Row, Row, Row Your Boat" and other rocking songs. Say "Ready, set, go," with a pause before *go*, before you start.

What is your baby learning?

As well as being soothing, this activity leads to confidence with movement and helps to develop awareness of space.

WHAT TO DO:

1. Fold the blanket in half to make a rectangle and lay it on the mat. Place your baby gently on the blanket and gather up two corners each to make a high-sided hammock.
2. Gently lift your baby in the blanket. With a soft and smooth action, swing the baby side to side and sing,

   Swinging, swinging, to and fro,
   This is just the way we go.
   Rocking, rocking, side to side
   Giving baby his first ride.

3. The tune to "Twinkle Twinkle Little Star" works, but you can always make up your own.
4. Gently lower the blanket down onto the mat.
5. Watch to see if your baby has enjoyed the activity. Offer, "Again?" Wait for some indication (a glance, a kick, a bounce, or maybe a sound) to tell you that you should repeat the song and the swing.

Another idea: Share the singing, or sing alternate lines. Try moving gently up and down as an alternative to swinging.

HELPFUL HINTS

Most children find swinging very comforting; this activity can be a good way of calming your baby down if he feels stressed. Think about how your baby lets you know what he wants.

Up the Arm, Down the Arm
a singing game

WHAT YOU NEED:

- a blanket, rug, or pile of cushions

WHAT TO DO:

1. Lay your baby on the floor on a blanket or rug. If you think she is likely to roll away, put a cushion on each side of her.
2. Gently hold one of your baby's hands so her arm is straight. "Walk" your other fingers up and down your baby's arm as you sing or say this song:

   Up your arm, up your arm,
   Walking up your arm.
   Down your arm, down your arm,
   Walking down your arm.

3. As you reach your baby's hand, give a tickle.
4. Watch to see if your baby has enjoyed the game. Offer "Again?" Wait for some indication, a glance, a kick, or maybe a sound to tell you that you should repeat the song and walking. This time, do it on the other arm.

Another idea: Sit your baby up and do the finger walking on her legs.

Gently, Gently
rock and sing

WHAT YOU NEED:

- No special equipment for this activity.

Ready for more?

Use ambient music and sound recordings (waves, water, quiet electronic music, and so on) to help provide rhythm and promote relaxation. When your baby is older, include a soft toy or teddy bear to join in the rocking and singing.

WHAT TO DO:

1. Find a quiet spot (a rocking chair, pile of cushions, or settee) and sit with your baby supported comfortably in your arms.
2. Look into your baby's eyes and gently rock him backward and forward.
3. Sing a quiet song. You could sing "Rock-a-Bye Baby," "Row, Row, Row Your Boat," or any favorite tune in a quiet voice. Gently stroke your baby's cheek as you sing or hum the tune.
4. If your baby reaches out to touch your face, move closer so you're in range.

Another idea: Play some soft music in the background.

HELPFUL HINTS

In fine weather do this activity outside, listening to the wind, watching the clouds, and watching the leaves. It doesn't have to be warm, so long as you both wrap up. Look at your baby a lot, and praise him when he looks at you. Eye contact is important.

What is your baby learning?

This activity helps with focus and eye development, as well as promoting a feeling of well-being. It leads to confidence, self-assurance, and trust.

What's Around?
exploring near you

WHAT YOU NEED:

- no special equipment, just a good eye for what your home offers

Ready for more?

Collect some objects in a basket. Place the basket in front of your baby, and let her choose which ones she's going to explore and play with. Some people call such a collection a "treasure basket." Encourage your baby to point to other objects she wants to look at. Bring these to her and praise her communication skills.

WHAT TO DO:

1. If your baby is young, carry her to different parts of the room to explore what's there. If your baby is older, encourage her to crawl.
2. Point to an object, name it, then pick it up and bring it near to her. Give an older crawler the chance to choose.
3. Talk about the object. Use words to say what it looks and feels like—for example, *lumpy, smooth, shiny.*
4. Encourage your baby to touch or hold the object by bringing it nearer.
5. Visit a different part of the room (or another room) to look at something else. Choose things that look and feel different from the first ones you picked—smooth/bumpy, shiny/matte, or soft and warm/cold and hard.

Another idea: If your baby is able to sit, settle her on the floor and bring objects for her to hold. Sit opposite her to talk about them.

What is your baby learning?

This activity is good preparation for imitating and comparing.

HELPFUL HINTS

Explore just two or three things to start with. Make sure the objects are small enough for your baby to see and hold, but not so small that they get dropped! Give your baby time to feel the objects—don't be in a hurry. One interesting object may hold her attention for some time.

DID YOU KNOW?

Babies have a definite preference for high contrast images, such as geometric shapes in black, white, and red.

Go the Hole Way!
exploring holes

WHAT YOU NEED:

- things with holes—sieves, colanders, plastic tea strainers, or plastic tubes
- whipped cream in a can
- slotted spoons and spatulas

WHAT TO DO:

1. Squeeze a small amount of cream into the colander and explore it with your baby, pushing it through the holes and experiencing the different textures.
2. Pat the cream with the spoons and spatulas, adding more cream as needed to keep the texture interesting.
3. Say or sing a simple commentary, using single words and short phrases. Describe how your baby is exploring the cream and holes, such as "Pat, pat, pat," "Push it in the hole," and "All gone."

Another idea: Put some cream on your baby's hands and play Pat-a-Cake.

DID YOU KNOW?

Some people think that babies are born without kneecaps. Babies do have kneecaps, but they are made of cartilage.

Ready for more?

If your baby is a little older (6 months+), encourage him to isolate his index fingers to make patterns in the cream or to poke into the holes. Spread sprinkles on a plastic tray and play at scattering them around.

What is your baby learning?

This activity helps develop hand and arm control and encourages exploration, investigation, and experimentation. It gives opportunities to explore cause and effect.

HELPFUL HINTS

Most young babies won't like cream on their faces and it could get in their eyes, so wipe it off. Most babies will put the cream in their mouths. Make sure everything is clean, and don't let them eat too much!

Index